MW00647503

The Family and
the Baby Whale

by Isaac Hales
illustrated by Rob Mancini

SCHOOL PUBLISHERS

Requests for permission to make copies of any part of the work should be addressed to School Permissions and Copyrights, Harcourt, Inc., 6277 Sea Harbor Drive, Orlando, Florida 32887–6777. Fax: 407-345-2418.

HARCOURT and the Harcourt Logo are trademarks of Harcourt, Inc., registered in the United States of America and/or other jurisdictions.

Printed in the United States of America

ISBN 10: 0-15-350393-9
ISBN 13: 978-0-15-350393-1

Ordering Options
ISBN 10: 0-15-350331-9 (Grade 1 Below-Level Collection)
ISBN 13: 978-0-15-350331-3 (Grade 1 Below-Level Collection)
ISBN 10: 0-15-357418-6 (package of 5)
ISBN 13: 978-0-15-357418-4 (package of 5)

2 3 4 5 6 7 8 9 10   179   15 14 13 12 11 10 09 08 07

Baby Whale was
playing in the sea. He
was swimming close to
the shore. Soon he was
no longer in the deep
water. His mother called
out to him to come back.

All of a sudden, Baby
Whale was trapped on
the sand.

"Look what he's done!"
his mother said.

She was sad because
she could not help him.

A family was walking
down the sand together.
They were splashing in
the pools left by the sea.
They had a pot for shells.

Then the family saw
Baby Whale on the sand.

"Look at that!" gasped
the children.

"It needs help," answered
their dad.

The children tipped
the shells out of the pot.
They filled it with water.
They kept Baby Whale
wet. People came to help.

They waited until the
waves came back in. Then
they pushed Baby Whale
out into the water.

Baby Whale called for his mother. He listened. Had his mother heard him?

Yes, she had. She was very pleased to see her baby. Baby Whale was more pleased to see her. Off they swam together.